Table of Contents

W9-AJU-363

continued on next page

© 1984, Instructional Fair, Inc.

continued from previous page

©1984, Instructional Fair, Inc.

Word Problems

Word Problems

Johnson City Flying Hawks					
Lead String			Reserves		
Name	Ht.	Wt.	Name	Ht.	Wt.
Schultz	5'3"	123	Jones	5'7"	140
Barton	5'8"	137	Ramsey	5'8"	132
Conway	5'10"	154	Morris	5'10"	151
Russell	5'8"	135	Watson	5'7"	135
Smith	5'9"	147	Black	5'6"	132

Figure the average height and weight of the Lead String players and of the Reserves. Then find the team averages.

Lead String   Reserves

53

Team Averages

Begin Step 1

© 1984, Instructional Fair, Inc.

1

Addition and Subtraction

Find the Sums

Check by subtracting.

```
  1
  785                 1,281
+ 496               -  496
  1,281                785
```

```
  438                1,264
+ 826                  826
  1,264                438
```

```
  953                1,717
+ 764                  764
  1,717                953
```

```
  749                1,091
+ 352                  352
  1,101                749
```

```
  1,625               6,361
+ 4,736               4,736
  6,361               1,625
```

Addition and Subtraction

Find the Sums

Check by subtracting.

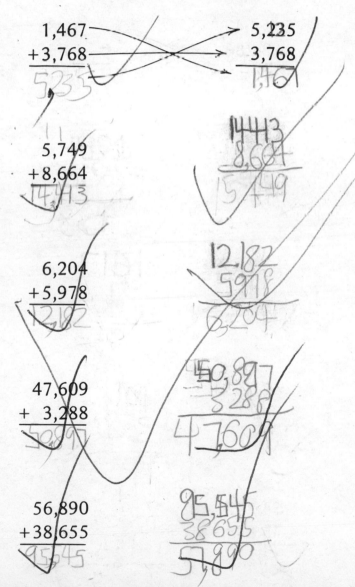

1,467
+3,768
_____
5235

5,235
3,768
_____
1,467

5,749
+8,664
_____
14413

14413
8,664
_____
15749

6,204
+5,978
_____
12182

12,182
5978
_____
6,204

47,609
+ 3,288
_____
50897

50,897
3,288
_____
47609

56,890
+38,655
_____
95545

95,545
38655
_____
57890

Subtraction and Addition

Find the Differences

Check by adding.

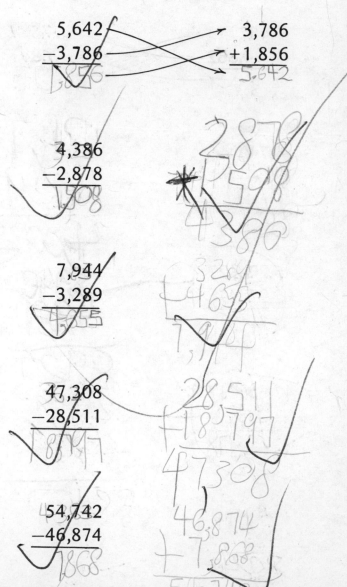

$$\begin{array}{r} 5,642 \\ -3,786 \\ \hline 1856 \end{array} \qquad \begin{array}{r} 3,786 \\ +1,856 \\ \hline 5,642 \end{array}$$

$$\begin{array}{r} 4,386 \\ -2,878 \\ \hline 1508 \end{array}$$

$$\begin{array}{r} 7,944 \\ -3,289 \\ \hline 4655 \end{array}$$

$$\begin{array}{r} 47,308 \\ -28,511 \\ \hline 18847 \end{array}$$

$$\begin{array}{r} 54,742 \\ -46,874 \\ \hline 7868 \end{array}$$

Subtraction and Addition

Find the Differences

Check by adding.

$$
\begin{array}{r}
8,743 \\
-4,862 \\
\hline
3,881
\end{array}
\qquad
\begin{array}{r}
4,862 \\
+3,881 \\
\hline
8,743
\end{array}
$$

$$
\begin{array}{r}
4,006 \\
-2,147 \\
\hline
1,859
\end{array}
$$

$$
\begin{array}{r}
8,927 \\
-3,946 \\
\hline
4,981
\end{array}
$$

$$
\begin{array}{r}
58,737 \\
-21,859 \\
\hline
36,878
\end{array}
$$

$$
\begin{array}{r}
40,008 \\
-19,759 \\
\hline
20,249
\end{array}
$$

5

Addition

Find the Sums

4	6	9	2	8	5
8	7	4	5	3	7
7	8	5	4	7	3
+6	+4	+2	+9	+5	+8

56	52	79	92
49	38	31	47
38	49	47	31
+52	+56	+92	+79

358	308	592	876
475	247	128	349
247	475	349	128
+308	+358	+876	+592

821	107	666	417
476	342	343	728
342	476	728	343
+107	+821	+417	+666

Addition and Multiplication

Whole and Mixed Numbers

Find the sums and products.

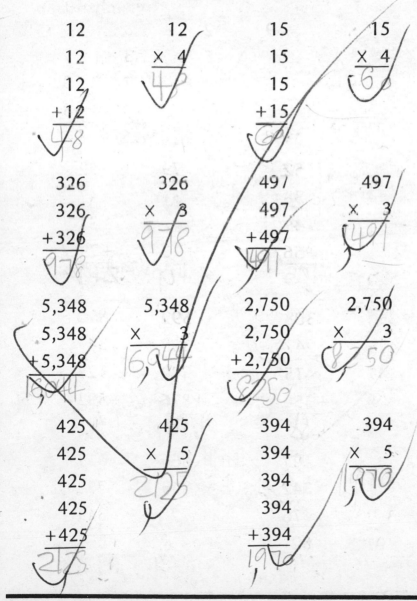

```
  12            12          15            15
  12          ×  4          15          ×  4
  12           48           15           60
+ 12                      + 15
  48                        60
```

```
  326           326         497           497
  326         ×   3         497         ×   3
+ 326           978       + 497           491
  978                       491
```

```
  5,348         5,348       2,750         2,750
  5,348       ×     3       2,750       ×     3
+ 5,348        16,044     + 2,750         8,250
  18,044                    8,250
```

```
  425           425         394           394
  425         ×   5         394         ×   5
  425          2125         394          1,970
  425                       394
+ 425                     + 394
  2125                      1,970
```

7

Weight Watching

Figure the weight of

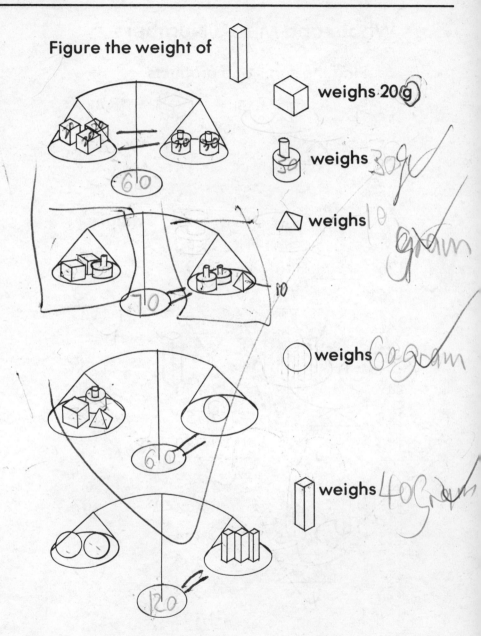

weighs 20g

weighs 30g

weighs 10 gram

weighs 60 gram

weighs 40 gram

Weight Watching

Figure the weight of the △

⬓ weighs 50 g

◯ weighs 25g

⬭ weighs 75g

▯ weighs 25g

△ weighs 15g

Number Sentences

Fill the blanks so that all of the number sentences are true.

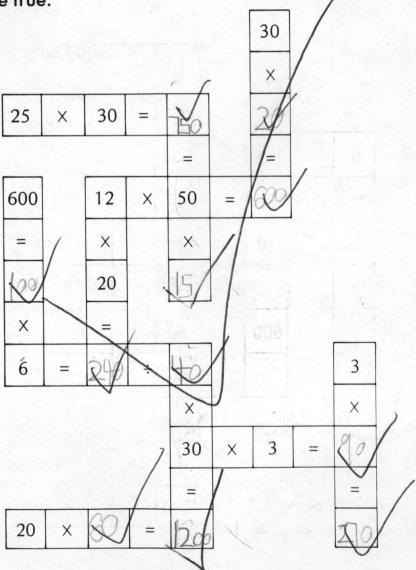

25 × 30 = 750

600 = 12 × 50 = 600

100 × 6 = 240 ÷ 40

30 × 3 = 90

20 × 60 = 120

30, 20, 15, 20, 3, 270

10

Number Sentences

Fill the blanks so that all of the number sentences are true.

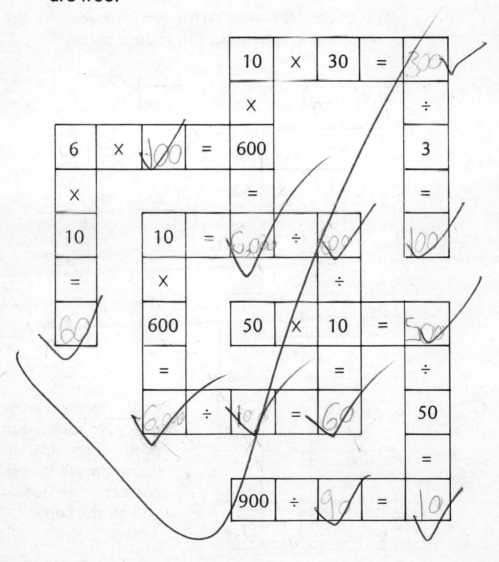

$10 \times 30 = 300$

$6 \times 100 = 600$

$10 \quad 10 = 600 \div 600 \quad 100$

$600 \quad 50 \times 10 = 500$

$6{,}000 \div 100 = 60 \quad 50$

$900 \div 90 = 10$

The Homework Booklet · © 1984, Instructional Fair, Inc.

Division Tic-Tac-Toe

Math Puzzles

Work each problem. Write the answers in the corresponding spaces on the square below.

a.
13 ⟌ 78

b.
46 ⟌ 46

c.
34 ⟌ 272

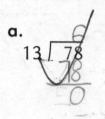

d.
67 ⟌ 469

e.
48 ⟌ 240

f.
16 ⟌ 48

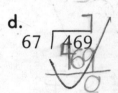

g.
59 ⟌ 118

h.
27 ⟌ 243

i.
19 ⟌ 76

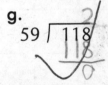
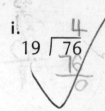

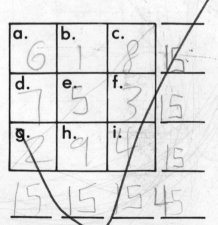

a.	b.	c.	
6	1	8	15
d.	e.	f.	
7	5	3	15
g.	h.	i.	
2	9	4	15
15	15	15	45

Add every row, every column, and both diagonals. If your answers are correct, all totals will be the same.

The Homework Booklet

Multiplication and Division

Find the Products

Check by dividing.

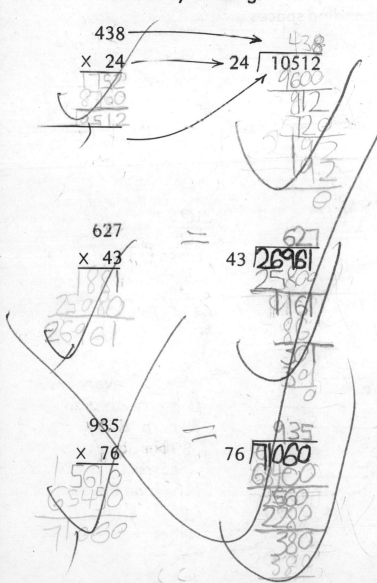

$$438 \times 24$$

$$24 \overline{)10512}$$

$$627 \times 43$$

$$43 \overline{)26961}$$

$$935 \times 76$$

$$76 \overline{)71060}$$

Multiplication and Division

Find the Products

Check by dividing.

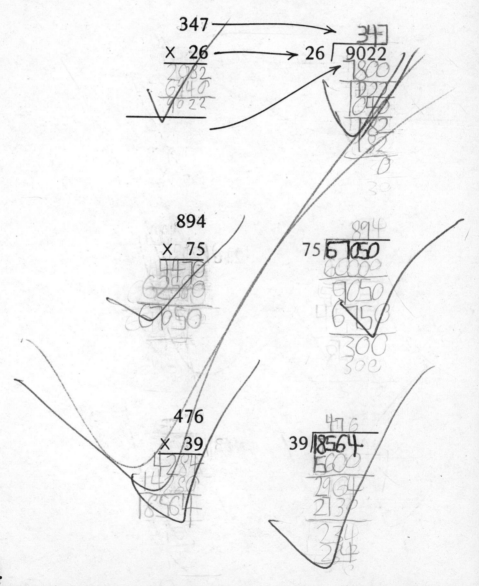

$$
\begin{array}{r} 347 \\ \times\ 26 \end{array}
\qquad
26\,\overline{)\,9022}
$$

$$
\begin{array}{r} 894 \\ \times\ 75 \end{array}
\qquad
75\,\overline{)\,67050}
$$

$$
\begin{array}{r} 476 \\ \times\ 39 \end{array}
\qquad
39\,\overline{)\,18564}
$$

14

Multiplication and Division

Find the Products

Check by dividing.

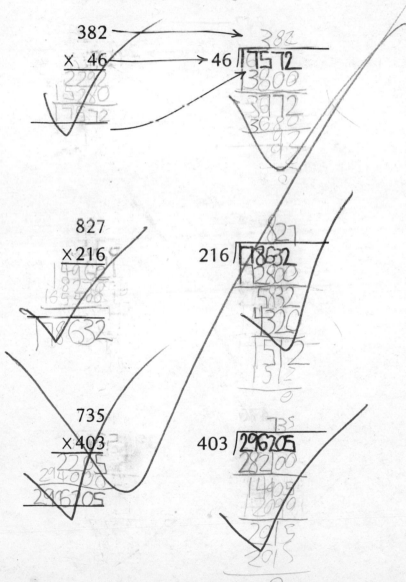

382
X 46

46 ⟌ 17572

827
X 216

216 ⟌ 178632

735
X 403

403 ⟌ 296205

Multiplication and Division

Find the Products

Check by dividing.

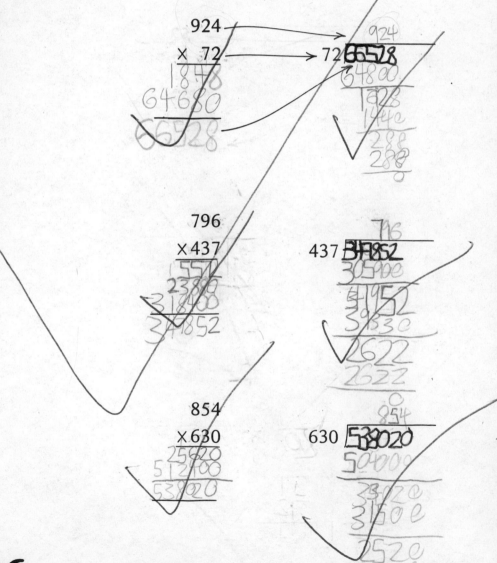

$$924 \times 72$$

$$796 \times 437$$

$$854 \times 630$$

Division and Multiplication

Find the Quotients

Check by multiplying.

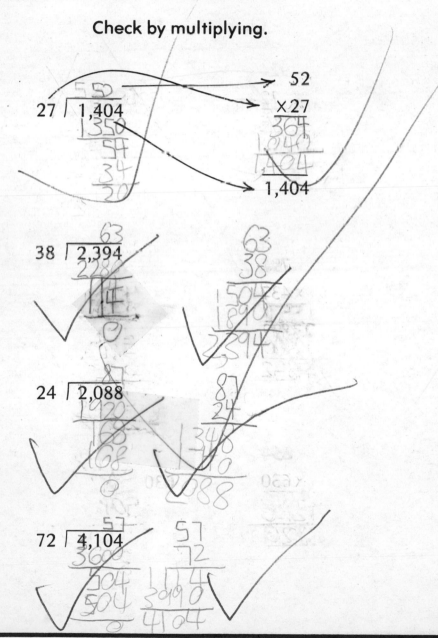

$$27 \overline{\smash{\big)}\,1{,}404} \qquad \begin{array}{r} 52 \\ \times 27 \\ \hline 364 \\ 1040 \\ \hline 1{,}404 \end{array}$$

$$38 \overline{\smash{\big)}\,2{,}394}$$

$$24 \overline{\smash{\big)}\,2{,}088}$$

$$72 \overline{\smash{\big)}\,4{,}104}$$

Division and Multiplication

Find the Quotients

Check by multiplying.

$$46 \overline{)1{,}058}$$

23
×46

$$63 \overline{)5{,}985}$$

$$18 \overline{)1{,}476}$$

$$84 \overline{)6{,}132}$$

The Homework Booklet   ©1984, Instructional Fair, Inc.

Division and Multiplication

Find the Quotients

Check by multiplying.

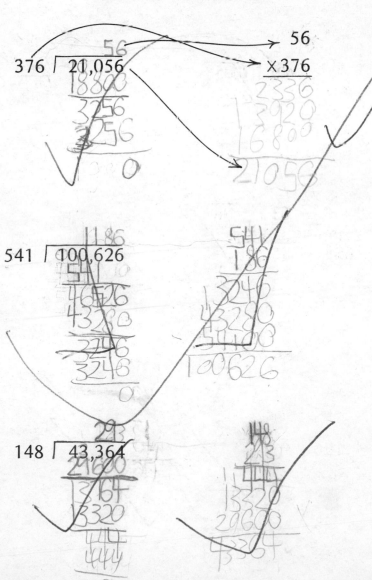

376 | 21,056

56
× 376

541 | 100,626

148 | 43,364

Division and Multiplication

Find the Quotients

Check by multiplying.

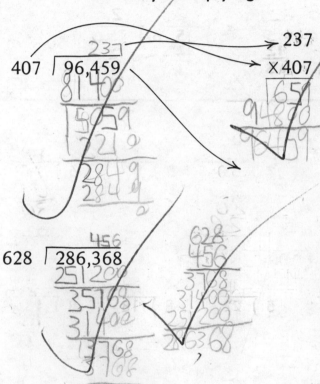

$$407 \overline{\smash{)}96{,}459}$$

$$237 \times 407$$

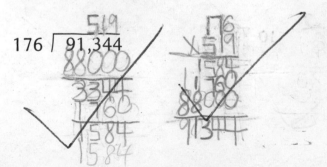

$$628 \overline{\smash{)}286{,}368}$$

$$176 \overline{\smash{)}91{,}344}$$

You have finished

Step 1

20

Decimals and Fractions

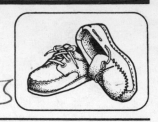

—11 points

Find the quotient as a fraction and as a decimal. Reduce fractions where necessary.

$$
\begin{array}{ccccc}
\,2 & 2\tfrac{3}{6}=2\tfrac{1}{2} & \,2 & \,2. & \,2.5 \\
6\,)\,\overline{15} & 6\,)\,\overline{15} & 6\,)\,\overline{15} & 6\,)\,\overline{15.0} & 6\,)\,\overline{15.0} \\
\underline{12} & \underline{12} & \underline{12} & \underline{12} & \underline{12} \\
\,3 & \,3 & \,3 & 30 & 30 \\
& & & & \underline{30} \\
\end{array}
$$

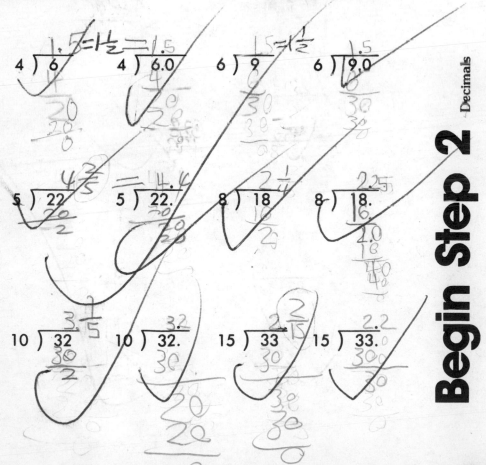

$$
4\,)\,\overline{6} \qquad 4\,)\,\overline{6.0} \qquad 6\,)\,\overline{9} \qquad 6\,)\,\overline{9.0}
$$

$$
5\,)\,\overline{22} \qquad 5\,)\,\overline{22.} \qquad 8\,)\,\overline{18} \qquad 8\,)\,\overline{18.}
$$

$$
10\,)\,\overline{32} \qquad 10\,)\,\overline{32.} \qquad 15\,)\,\overline{33} \qquad 15\,)\,\overline{33.}
$$

Begin Step 2 — Decimals

21

Decimals and Fractions

— 6 points + 1 points

Find the quotient as a fraction and as a decimal. Reduce fractions where necessary.

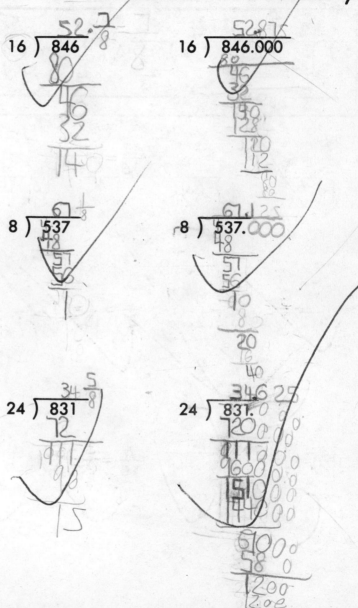

$$16 \overline{)846}$$

$$16 \overline{)846.000}$$

$$8 \overline{)537}$$

$$8 \overline{)537.000}$$

$$24 \overline{)831}$$

$$24 \overline{)831.0}$$

©1984, Instructional Fair, Inc.

Decimals and Fractions

Reduce each fraction to lowest terms and convert to the decimal form.

$$\frac{9}{18} = \frac{1}{2}$$

$2 \overline{)1.}$

$2 \overline{)\begin{array}{r} .5 \\ 1.0 \\ 1 \ 0 \\ \hline 0 \end{array}}$

Study this first

$\frac{4}{16} = \frac{1}{4} = .25$

$\frac{12}{16} = \frac{3}{4} = .75$

$\frac{10}{16} = \frac{5}{8} = .625$

$\frac{3}{24} = \frac{1}{8} = .125$

$\frac{14}{16} = \frac{7}{8} = .875$

$\frac{6}{16} = \frac{3}{8} = .375$

Decimals and Fractions

─2points

1 point

Convert each fraction to decimal form. Round decimals to nearest thousandth if necessary.

$$\frac{7}{9} = 9\overline{)7.0}$$

$$9\overline{)7.0} \quad .7777 = .778$$
$$\underline{63}$$
$$70$$
$$\underline{63}$$
$$70$$
$$\underline{63}$$
$$70$$
$$\underline{63}$$
$$7$$

$$\frac{1}{3} = 3\overline{)10} \quad .3333$$

$$\frac{5}{6} = 6\overline{)5.00} \quad .833$$

$$\frac{2}{7} = 7\overline{)20} \quad .2857$$

$$\frac{1}{12} = 12\overline{)00} \quad .0833$$

Decimals and Fractions

– 3 points
+ 1 point

Find the decimal form of each fraction and write it as a word statement.

fraction	decimal	word statement
$\frac{7}{10}$ =	$10\overline{)\begin{array}{c} .7 \\ 7.0 \\ 7.0 \end{array}}$ =	seven tenths

$\frac{4}{8}$ = $8\overline{)\begin{array}{c} .5 \\ 40 \\ 40 \\ \overline{0} \end{array}}$ = five tenths

$\frac{8}{10}$ = $10\overline{)\begin{array}{c} .8 \\ 80 \\ 80 \\ \overline{0} \end{array}}$ = eight tenths

$\frac{2}{8}$ = $8\overline{)\begin{array}{c} .25 \\ 20 \\ 16 \\ 40 \\ 40 \\ \overline{0} \end{array}}$ = twenty-five hundredths

$\frac{3}{4}$ = $4\overline{)\begin{array}{c} .75 \\ 300 \\ 28 \\ 20 \\ 20 \\ \overline{0} \end{array}}$ = Seventy-five hundredths

25

© 1984, Instructional Fair, Inc.

Decimals and Fractions

How to start

Find the decimal form of each fraction and write it as a word statement.

$$\frac{3}{8} = 8\overline{)\begin{array}{c} .375 \\ 3.000 \end{array}} = \text{three hundred seventy-five thousandths}$$

$$\begin{array}{r} 2.4 \\ \hline 60 \\ 56 \\ \hline 40 \end{array}$$

fraction   decimal   word statement

$$\frac{7}{8} = 8\overline{)\begin{array}{c} .875 \\ 7.000 \end{array}} = \text{eight hundred seventy-five thousandths}$$

$$\begin{array}{r} 64 \\ \hline 60 \\ 56 \\ \hline 40 \\ 40 \\ \hline 0 \end{array}$$

$$\frac{9}{24} = 24\overline{)\begin{array}{c} .375 \\ 9.000 \end{array}} = \text{three hundred seventy-five thousandths.}$$

$$\begin{array}{r} 7.2 \\ \hline 1800 \\ 168 \\ \hline 120 \\ 120 \\ \hline 0 \end{array}$$

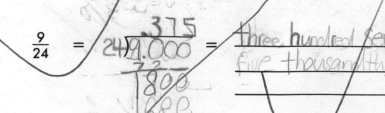

The Homework Booklet

Equivalents

−8 points

an example

Fill in the percent equivalent.

$\frac{1}{4}$	=	.25	=	25%

fraction		decimal		percent
$\frac{1}{2}$	=	.5	=	50%
$\frac{3}{5}$	=	.6	=	60%
$\frac{4}{5}$	=	.8	=	80%
$\frac{7}{10}$	=	.70	=	70%
$\frac{11}{20}$	=	.55	=	55%
$\frac{1}{3}$	=	$.33\frac{1}{3}$	=	$33\frac{1}{3}%$
$\frac{5}{6}$	=	$.83\frac{1}{3}$	=	$83\frac{1}{3}%$
$\frac{3}{8}$	=	.375	=	37.5%
$\frac{1}{20}$	=	.05	=	5%

27

Equivalents

Fill in the missing equivalents.

$$\frac{2}{5} \quad = \quad .4 \quad = \quad 40\%$$

fraction		decimal		percent
$\frac{1}{3}$	=	$33\frac{1}{3}$	=	$33\frac{1}{3}\%$
	=	.5	=	50%
	=		=	25%
$\frac{1}{6}$	=	$16\frac{2}{3}$	=	$16\frac{2}{3}\%$
$\frac{5}{6}$	=	$.83\frac{1}{3}$	=	$83\frac{1}{3}\%$
	=		=	75%
$\frac{7}{8}$	=	$.875$	=	87.5%
	=	.1	=	10%
	=	$.65$	=	65%

Equivalents

-2 points

Show the decimal equivalent to the mixed number.

| $3\frac{4}{5}$ | = | $3.000 + .800$ | = | 3.800 |

$4\frac{1}{5}$ = $4.000 + 0.200$ = 4.200

$9\frac{3}{8}$ = $9.000 + .375$ = 9.375

$5\frac{4}{5}$ = $5.000 + 0.800$ = 5.800

$6\frac{1}{10}$ = $6.000 + 0.100$ = 6.100

$3\frac{5}{8}$ = $3.000 + .625$ = 3.625

$2\frac{3}{4}$ = $2.000 + 0.75$ = 2.750

$8\frac{7}{10}$ = $8.000 + 0.700$ = 8.700

$3\frac{19}{20}$ = $3.000 + 0.95$ = 3.95

$7\frac{3}{20}$ = $7.000 + 0.15$ = 7.150

29

© 1984, Instructional Fair, Inc.

Equivalents

— (point

Show the decimal equivalent to the mixed number.

$$35\frac{1}{1000} = 35.000 + .001 = 35.001$$

$73\frac{1}{5}$ = 73.000+0.2 = 73.200

$27\frac{4}{5}$ = 27.000+0.8 = 27.800

$52\frac{4}{10}$ = 52.000+0.4 = 52.400

$93\frac{3}{10}$ = 93.000+0.3 = 93.300

$39\frac{1}{25}$ = 39.000+0.04 = 39.040

$51\frac{1}{50}$ = 51.000+0.02 = 51.020

$65\frac{7}{100}$ = 65.000+0.07 = 65.070

$83\frac{126}{1000}$ = 83.000+.126 = 83.126

$48\frac{21}{1000}$ = 48.000+00.021 = 48.021

30

Math Puzzles

Choose the greater of each pair and record that number in the corresponding space on the square below.

a. $\frac{2}{5}$, .39 $= .39$

$= .4$

b. $\frac{11}{13}$, .9

$= .846$

c. $\frac{1}{5}$, .05 $= .05$

$= .2$

d. $\frac{1}{10}$, .3

$= .1$

e. $\frac{1}{2}$, .43

$= .5$

f. $\frac{2}{3}$, .7 $=$

$= .66$

g. $\frac{4}{5}$, .7

$= .8$

h. $\frac{2}{21}$, .1

$= .09$

i. $\frac{4}{7}$, .6

$.57$

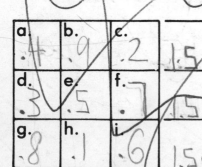

a. .4	b. .9	c. .2	1.5
d. .3	e. .5	f. .7	1.5
g. .8	h. .1	i. .6	1.5
1.5	1.5	1.5	4.5

Add every row, every column, and both diagonals. If your answers are correct, all totals will be the same.

31

Decimals and Fractions

~ 8 points

Arrange the values in ascending order.

Here's an example

.75	$\frac{1}{2}$	35%	.6
.35%	$\frac{1}{2}$	.6	.75

.77	50% = .5	.21	$\frac{1}{4}$ = .25
.21	$\frac{1}{4}$	50%	.77

80% = .8	.38	$\frac{7}{20}$ = .35	40% = .4
$\frac{7}{20}$	.38	40%	.8

52%	.48	$\frac{1}{2}$ = .5	.53
.48	$\frac{1}{2}$	52%	.53

.76	$\frac{7}{8}$ = .875	72%	$\frac{3}{4}$ = .75
72%	$\frac{3}{4}$	.76	$\frac{7}{8}$

The Homework Booklet ©1984, Instructional Fair, Inc.

Percentages

Find ⅓% of 40. $= \frac{4}{10} = \frac{2}{5} = \frac{2}{5}$

$= \frac{1}{3} \times \frac{2}{5} = \frac{2}{15} = .133$

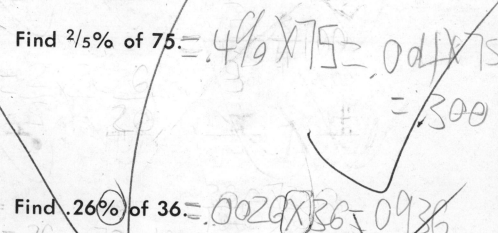

Find .6% of 82. $= 82 \times \frac{.6}{100} = 82 \times .006$

$\frac{6}{100} \times \frac{41}{50}$ $= .492$

Find ⅖% of 75. $= .4\% \times 75 = .004 \times 75$

$= .300$

Find .26% of 36. $= .0026 \times 36 = .0936$

33

Decimals and Fractions

— 7 points

Arrange the values in ascending order.

.3	$\frac{7}{10}$	.08	35%
.08	.3	35%	$\frac{7}{10}$

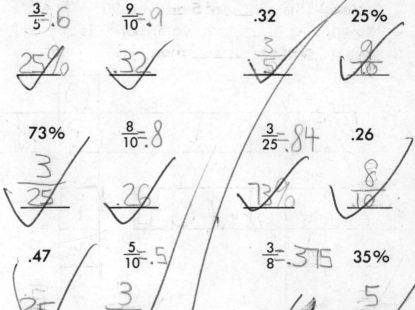

$\frac{3}{5}$ .6	$\frac{9}{10}$ .9	.32	25%
25%	.32	$\frac{3}{5}$	$\frac{9}{10}$

73%	$\frac{8}{10}$ .8	$\frac{3}{25}$ .84	.26
$\frac{3}{25}$	.26	73%	$\frac{8}{10}$

.47	$\frac{5}{10}$ .5	$\frac{3}{8}$ .375	35%
35%	$\frac{3}{8}$	.47	$\frac{5}{10}$

.68	$\frac{5}{8}$ = .625	67%	$\frac{26}{50}$ = .484
$\frac{26}{50}$	$\frac{5}{8}$	67%	.68

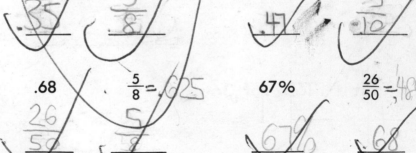

34

Crosswords

Write the word that corresponds to each clue on the correct spaces on the puzzle.

1. The _____ equivalent of ¼ is .25.
2. .50 is the decimal _____ of ½.
3. The _____ of 2 into 14 is 7.
4. (across) The _____ of 5 and 4 is 20.
4. (down) The _____ equivalent of ¼ is 25%.
5. ½ has a greater _____ than ⅓.

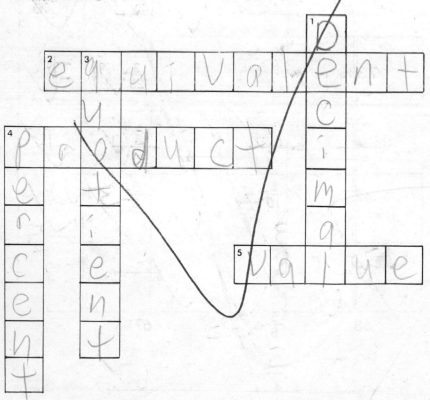

© 1984, Instructional Fair, Inc.

Number Table

Complete the Table

+	7.3	.04	6.72	9	1.38
.54	7.84	.58	7.26	9.54	1.92
6.68	13.98	6.72	13.4	15.68	8.06
7.05	14.35	7.09	13.77	16.05	8.43
.95	8.25	.99	7.67	9.95	2.33
2.62	9.92	2.66	9.34	11.62	4

Math Puzzles

What solution is named most often? _____

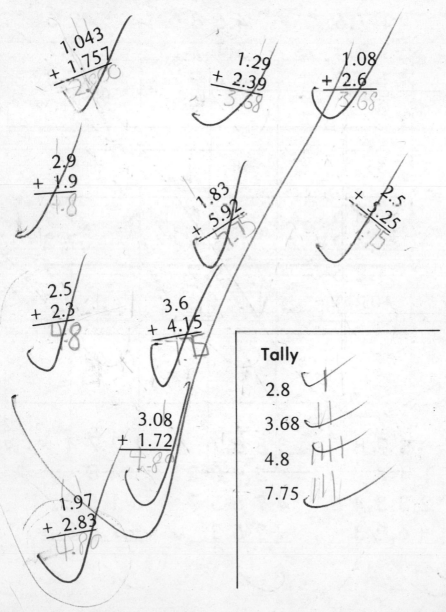

$$\begin{array}{r} 1.043 \\ + \ 1.757 \\ \hline \end{array}$$

$$\begin{array}{r} 1.29 \\ + \ 2.39 \\ \hline \end{array}$$

$$\begin{array}{r} 1.08 \\ + \ 2.6 \\ \hline \end{array}$$

$$\begin{array}{r} 2.9 \\ + \ 1.9 \\ \hline \end{array}$$

$$\begin{array}{r} 1.83 \\ + \ 5.92 \\ \hline \end{array}$$

$$\begin{array}{r} 2.5 \\ + \ 3.25 \\ \hline \end{array}$$

$$\begin{array}{r} 2.5 \\ + \ 2.3 \\ \hline \end{array}$$

$$\begin{array}{r} 3.6 \\ + \ 4.15 \\ \hline \end{array}$$

$$\begin{array}{r} 3.08 \\ + \ 1.72 \\ \hline \end{array}$$

$$\begin{array}{r} 1.97 \\ + \ 2.83 \\ \hline \end{array}$$

Tally

2.8

3.68

4.8

7.75

Decimals

Find the sums.

1 7.6	4.6 8	2.6
1 3.4	5.1 7	8.7
+1 8.2	+ 8.4 9	+9.3
49.2	18.34	20.6

.3 5	.7 6	.8 8
.4 9	.3 8	.7 2
.8 6	.9 9	.7 7
+.3 1	+.4 3	+.9 5
2.01	2.56	3.32

3.9 8	3 8 6.7	1 7.7 4
1 4.7	5 9.8 2	4.8
2 8.5 4 6	4 7 6.5 7	3 1.5 2
+6.8 3	+2 5.3	+7.6 8 5
54.056	948.39	61.745

Decimals

1 points

Copy the problems in columns and find the sums.

a. $53.68 + 487.2 + 8.468 = $ *549.348*

b. $3.784 + 8.92 + 6.88 + 8.752 = $ *28.336*

c. $17.6 + 49.483 + 6.852 = $ *73.935*

d. $.5 + .83 + .477 + .36 = $ *2.167*

a.
```
  5 3.6 8
4 8 7.2
 +8.4 6 8
```
549.348

b.

c.

d.

39

© 1984, Instructional Fair, Inc.

Decimal Tic-Tac-Toe

— 4 points

Math Puzzles

Work each problem. Write the answers in the corresponding spaces on the square below.

a. 3.2
  − 2.5
  ‾‾‾‾
   .7

b. .9
  + .8
  ‾‾‾‾
  1.7

c. 2.1
  − 1.8
  ‾‾‾‾
   .3

d. .34
  + .16
  ‾‾‾‾
   .50

e. .07
  + .83
  ‾‾‾‾
   .90

f. 9.1
  − 7.8
  ‾‾‾‾
  1.3

g. .76
  + .74
  ‾‾‾‾
  1.50

h. .42
  − .32
  ‾‾‾‾
   .10

i. .5
  + .6
  ‾‾‾‾
  1.1

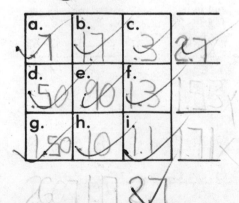

a. .7	b. .7	c. .3	2.7
d. .50	e. 90	f. 1.3	1.53
g. 1.50	h. .10	i. 1.1	1.71

2.6 2.7 1.7   2.7

Add every row, every column, and both diagonals. If your answers are correct, all totals will be the same.

40

©1984, Instructional Fair, Inc.

Decimals

0 point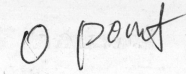

Find the differences.

```
  378.654        663.027
 -149.847       -187.539
  228.807        475.488


  476.314        897.347
 -287.225       -433.688
  189.089        463.659


  82.474    71.549    48.652
 -36.543   -67.223   -31.884
  45.931     4.326    16.768


  47.06     87.34     19.98
 -28.34    -29.76     -8.99
  18.72     57.58     10.99


  28.00     49.00     85.00
 -10.72    -16.86    -37.43
  17.28     32.14     47.57
```

41

Decimals

−2 points

Copy the problems in columns and find the differences.

a. 786.34 − 542.23 = 244.11

b. 590.687 − 426.78 = 163.907

c. 31.685 − 22.986 = 8.699

d. 7.639 − 2.887 = 4.752

a.

```
  7 8 6.3 4
− 5 4 2.2 3
  2 4 4.1 1
```

b.

c.

d.

Number Table

Complete the Table

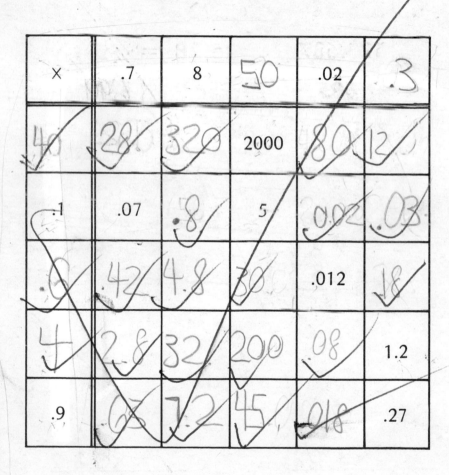

X	.7	8	50	.02	.3
40	28	320	2000	80	12
.1	.07	.8	5	0.02	.03
6	.42	4.8	30	.012	18
4	2.8	32	200	.08	1.2
.9	63	7.2	45	.018	.27

43

1 point

Decimals

Find the products.

$$\begin{array}{r} 428 \\ \times 3.7 \\ \hline 2996 \\ 1284 \\ \hline 583.6 \end{array}$$

$$\begin{array}{r} 519 \\ \times 4.7 \\ \hline 3633 \\ 2076 \\ \hline 2439.3 \end{array}$$

$$\begin{array}{r} 865 \\ \times .87 \\ \hline 6055 \\ 6920 \\ \hline 752.55 \end{array}$$

$$\begin{array}{r} 603 \\ \times .92 \\ \hline 1206 \\ 5427 \\ \hline 554.76 \end{array}$$

$$\begin{array}{r} 38.6 \\ \times 41.8 \\ \hline 3088 \\ 3860 \\ 15440 \\ \hline 1613.48 \end{array}$$

$$\begin{array}{r} 76.4 \\ \times 53.2 \\ \hline 1528 \\ 22920 \\ 38200 \\ \hline 4064.48 \end{array}$$

The Homework Booklet

Fred's Fresh Fruit

−1 point

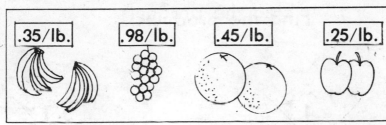

| .35/lb. | .98/lb. | .45/lb. | .25/lb. |

Figure the total costs of these purchases. Figure as much as you can in your head.

3.5 lb. apples
1 lb. grapes
3 lb. bananas

$.875
$.980
$.05
$2.705

6 lb. grapes
4 lb. apples
1 lb. oranges

$5.88
$1.00
$0.45
$7.33

2.8 lb. oranges
4 lb. apples
1.3 lb. grapes

$1.260
$1.00
$1.274
$3.53

Decimals

Find the products.

```
  4.7 2 9
× 5.3 6
```
25.34744

```
  8 6.4 3
× 3 2.8
```
2834904

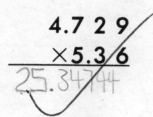

```
  8 3 0.6
× .1 9 6
```
162.7976

```
  7 5 4.9
× 4.6 3
```
3495.187

```
  5.2 7 4
× 5 8.4
```
308.0016

```
  2 9.4 6
× 8 0 3.
```
23656.38

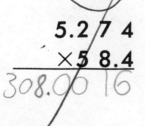

46

Percentages

— 1 point

Find 16% of 54.

$$
\begin{array}{r}
54 \\
\times\,.16 \\
\hline
324 \\
54 \\
\hline
8.64
\end{array}
$$

We did this one for you

Find 62% of 148.

$= .62 \times 148 = 91.76$

Find 47% of 112.

$= .47 \times 112 = 52.64$

Find 18% of 92.

$= .18 \times 92 = 16.56$

Find 26% of 52.

$= .26 \times 52 = 13.52$

47

— 3 *print* **Percentages**

At the Store

A record costs $5.98. How much do four records plus a sales tax of 4% total?

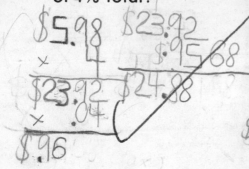

$5.98
× 4
$23.92
× .04
$.96

$23.92
$.95 68
$24.88

A pair of jeans costs $7.25. How much do four pairs of jeans plus a sales tax of 5% total?

$7.25
4
$29.00
.05
$1.45 00

$29.00
7.45 00
$30.45 00

A pound of apples costs 34¢. How much do 12 pounds of apples plus a sales tax of 3% total?

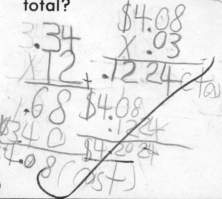

3.34
×12
.68
$34 0
$4.08 (cost)

$4.08
× .03
.12 24 ¢ (tax)
$4.08
.12 24
$4.20 24

A goldfish costs 85¢. How much do 12 gold-fish and a sales tax of 4% total?

85
× 12
1.70
8.50
$10.20 (costs)
.04
×

10.20
4080
$10.61

(tax) $.40 80

The Homework Booklet ©1984, Instructional Fair, Inc.

Percentages

Find 25% of $45.00.

$$
\begin{array}{r}
\$45.00 \\
\times .25 \\
\hline
22500 \\
9000 \\
\hline
\$11.2500
\end{array}
$$

an example

A × B = C. ?

Find 95% of $126.00. — 119.7000

Find 67% of $92.00. — 61.6400

Find 17% of $35.65. — 6.0605

Percentages

Number Sentences

Fill the blanks so that all of the number sentences are true.

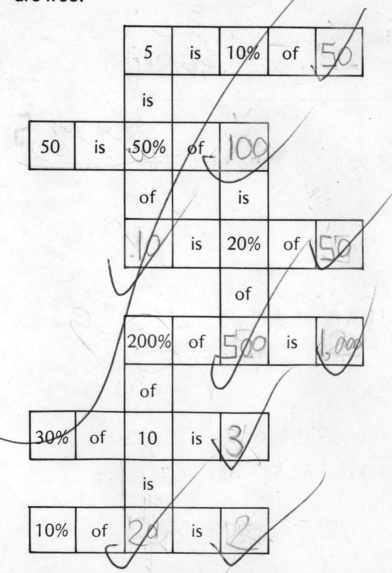

5	is	10%	of	50
	is			
50	is	50%	of	100
	of		is	
	10	is	20%	of	50
			of	
	200%	of	500	is	1,000
		of		
30%	of	10	is	3
		is		
10%	of	20	is	2

Percentages

Math Puzzles

What solution is named most often? _____

10% of 20 = 2

3% of 100 = 3

5% of 100 = 5

6% of 50 = 3

4% of 100 = 4

10% of 30 = 3

50% of 4 = 2

1% of 200 = 2

5% of 80 = 4

20% of 10 = 2

Tally	
2 =	IIII
3 =	III
4 =	II
5 =	I

Percentages

Food Prices

A grocery store pays $ .36 per loaf for a certain type of bread. They sell the same bread for $ .59 per loaf. Figure the percentage of profit on the bread.

A piece of meat weighed 1.9 kg before it was cooked and only 1.1 kg after it was cooked to a certain point. Figure the percentage of weight lost in cooking.

At one time a bottle of soda pop cost $ .05. Now the same size bottle costs $ .25. Figure the percentage of increase in cost.

52

Decimals

Find the quotients.

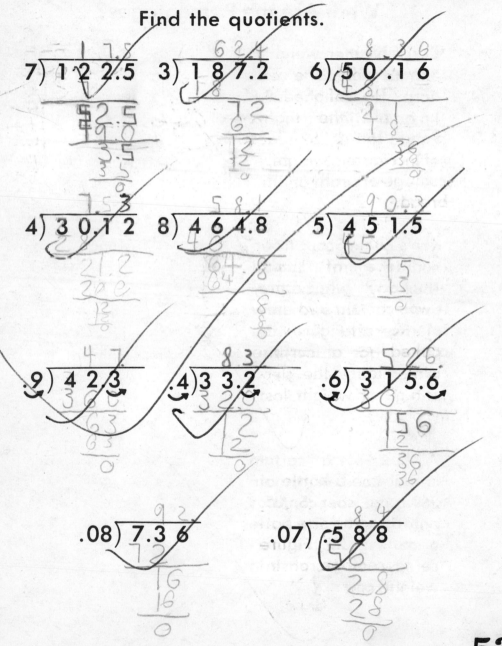

$$7\overline{)122.5} \qquad 3\overline{)187.2} \qquad 6\overline{)50.16}$$

$$4\overline{)30.12} \qquad 8\overline{)464.8} \qquad 5\overline{)451.5}$$

$$.9\overline{)42.3} \qquad .4\overline{)33.2} \qquad .6\overline{)315.6}$$

$$.08\overline{)7.36} \qquad .07\overline{).588}$$

53

© 1984, Instructional Fair, Inc.

Percentages

3 points

What Are the Percentages?

Chris' brother weighed 3.2 kg when he was born. He weighed 9.8 kg on his first birthday. Figure the percentages of increase in weight.

$$2.06 \times \frac{100}{100} = \frac{206}{100} = 206\%$$

Ken's Eagle Scout troop had 16 members until Thursday when they gained (three) new members. Figure the percentage of increase in membership.

$$.188 \times \frac{100}{100} = \frac{18.8}{100} = 18.8\%$$

A box of a certain cereal used to contain 369 g but now contains only 350 g for the same price. Figure the percentage of decrease in weight.

$$.05 \times \frac{100}{100} = \frac{5}{100} = 5\%$$

54

Decimals

1 point

Find the quotients.

```
          8.2                        .63
   .47) 3.8 5 4            .8 5) 5.3 5 5
                                 5 1 0
          9 4                     2 5 5
          9 4                     2 5 5
            0                         0
```

```
          6 9                         3
  .0 3 6) .2 4 8 4          .0 4 2) .1 5 5 4
          2 1 6                    1 2 6
          3 2 4                    2 9 4
          3 2 4                    2 9 4
            0
```

```
          3 8.6                      6 4
  .0 8 8) 3.3 9 6 8         .1 3 7) 8.7 6 8
          2 6 4                    8 2 2
          1 5 6 8                    5 4 8
          7 0 4                      5 4 8
            5 2 8                        0
            5 2 8
              0
```

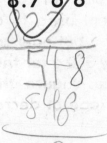

You have finished

Step 2

55

— (point **Fractions**

Find the Sums

Reduce your answers to lowest terms when necessary.

Begin Step 3

$$\frac{7}{8} = \frac{7}{8}$$
$$+ \frac{1}{2} = \frac{4}{8}$$
$$\frac{11}{8}$$

$$\frac{3}{4} = \frac{3}{4}$$
$$+ \frac{1}{2} = \frac{2}{4}$$
$$\frac{5}{4}$$

$$\frac{3}{5} = \frac{6}{10}$$
$$+ \frac{1}{2} = \frac{5}{10}$$
$$\frac{11}{10}$$

$$\frac{4}{5} = \frac{2}{5}$$
$$\frac{2}{3} = \frac{10}{15}$$
$$+ \frac{4}{15} = \frac{4}{15}$$
$$\frac{26}{15}$$

$$\frac{2}{3} = \frac{4}{6}$$
$$+ \frac{1}{2} = \frac{3}{6}$$
$$\frac{7}{6}$$

$$\frac{1}{2} = \frac{7}{4}$$
$$+ \frac{6}{7} = \frac{12}{14}$$
$$\frac{19}{14}$$

$$\frac{5}{8} = \frac{15}{24}$$
$$+ \frac{2}{3} = \frac{16}{24}$$
$$\frac{31}{24}$$

$$\frac{2}{3} = \frac{28}{42}$$
$$\frac{4}{7} = \frac{24}{42}$$
$$+ \frac{1}{2} = \frac{21}{42}$$
$$\frac{73}{42}$$

56

Fractions

−2 points

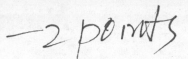

Find the Sums

Reduce your answers to lowest terms when necessary.

$\dfrac{7}{8} = \dfrac{7}{8}$

$+ \dfrac{3}{4} = \dfrac{6}{8}$

$\dfrac{13}{8} = 1\dfrac{5}{8}$

$\dfrac{1}{3} = \dfrac{2}{6}$

$+ \dfrac{5}{6} = \dfrac{5}{6}$

$\dfrac{7}{6} = 1\dfrac{1}{6}$

$\dfrac{4}{5} = \dfrac{8}{10}$

$+ \dfrac{1}{2} = \dfrac{5}{10}$

$\dfrac{13}{10} = 1\dfrac{3}{10}$

$\dfrac{3}{8} = \dfrac{21}{28}$

$+ \dfrac{2}{3} = \dfrac{16}{24}$

$\dfrac{37}{24} = 1\dfrac{13}{24}$

$\dfrac{2}{3} = \dfrac{14}{2}$

$+ \dfrac{5}{7} = \dfrac{15}{21}$

$\dfrac{29}{21} = 1\dfrac{8}{21}$

$\dfrac{4}{5} = \dfrac{12}{15}$

$+ \dfrac{1}{3} = \dfrac{5}{15}$

$\dfrac{17}{15} = 1\dfrac{2}{15}$

$\dfrac{7}{8} = \dfrac{21}{24}$

$\dfrac{2}{3} = \dfrac{16}{24}$

$+ \dfrac{11}{12} = \dfrac{22}{24}$

$\dfrac{59}{24} = 2\dfrac{11}{24}$

$\dfrac{3}{5} = \dfrac{18}{30}$

$\dfrac{5}{6} = \dfrac{25}{30}$

$+ \dfrac{7}{10} = \dfrac{21}{30}$

$\dfrac{64}{30} = 2\dfrac{4}{30} = 2\dfrac{2}{15}$

57

Number Table

Complete the Table

+	$\frac{1}{2}$	$\frac{2}{3}$	$\frac{3}{5}$	$\frac{1}{6}$	$\frac{3}{4}$
$\frac{3}{4}$		$1\frac{5}{12}$	$\frac{7}{20}$	$\frac{11}{12}$	$\frac{1}{2}$
$\frac{1}{5}$	$\frac{7}{10}$	$\frac{13}{15}$	$\frac{4}{5}$	$\frac{11}{30}$	$\frac{19}{20}$
$\frac{1}{2}$	1	$\frac{1}{6}$	$1\frac{1}{10}$	$\frac{2}{3}$	$\frac{1}{4}$
$\frac{1}{4}$	$\frac{3}{4}$	$\frac{11}{12}$	$\frac{17}{20}$	$\frac{5}{12}$	1
$\frac{2}{3}$	$\frac{1}{6}$	$1\frac{1}{3}$	$\frac{4}{5}$	$\frac{5}{6}$	$1\frac{5}{12}$

Fractions

Find the Sums

Reduce your answers to lowest terms when necessary.

$$\begin{array}{r} 3\dfrac{1}{3} = \dfrac{5}{15} \\ + \ 2\dfrac{4}{5} = \dfrac{12}{15} \\ \hline 5 \qquad \dfrac{17}{15} = 1\dfrac{2}{15} \\ 6\dfrac{2}{15} \end{array}$$

Your example

$$\begin{array}{r} 2\dfrac{1}{2} \ \dfrac{4}{8} \\ + \ 3\dfrac{3}{8} \ \dfrac{3}{8} \\ \hline 5\dfrac{7}{8} \end{array}$$

$$\begin{array}{r} 4\dfrac{5}{6} \ \dfrac{5}{6} \\ + \ 3\dfrac{1}{3} \ \dfrac{2}{6} \\ \hline 7\dfrac{7}{6} \ 8\dfrac{1}{6} \end{array}$$

$$\begin{array}{r} 2\dfrac{3}{4} \ \dfrac{15}{20} \\ 3\dfrac{1}{5} \ \dfrac{4}{20} \\ + \ 6\dfrac{2}{5} \ \dfrac{8}{20} \\ \hline 11\dfrac{27}{20} = 12\dfrac{7}{20} \end{array}$$

$$\begin{array}{r} 9\dfrac{3}{5} \ 9\dfrac{18}{30} \\ 5\dfrac{1}{3} \ \dfrac{10}{30} \\ + \ 7\dfrac{9}{10} \ 7\dfrac{27}{30} \\ \hline 21\dfrac{55}{30} = 21\dfrac{11}{6} = 22\dfrac{5}{6} \end{array}$$

$$\begin{array}{r} 18\dfrac{1}{6} \ 18\dfrac{4}{24} \\ 33\dfrac{7}{8} \ 33\dfrac{21}{24} \\ + \ 19\dfrac{11}{12} \ 19\dfrac{22}{24} \\ \hline 70\dfrac{47}{24} = 71\dfrac{23}{24} \end{array}$$

$$\begin{array}{r} 37\dfrac{5}{7} \ \dfrac{45}{63} \\ 46\dfrac{7}{9} \ \dfrac{49}{63} \\ + \ 13\dfrac{2}{3} \ \dfrac{42}{63} \\ \hline 96\dfrac{136}{63} = 98\dfrac{10}{63} \end{array}$$

Math Puzzles

What solution is named most often? _____

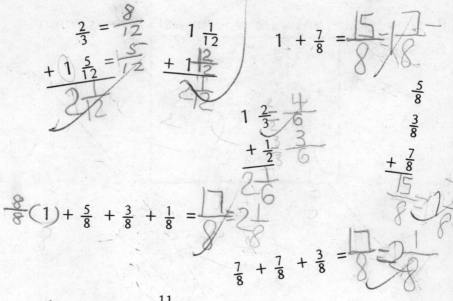

$$\frac{2}{3} = \frac{8}{12}$$
$$+ 1\frac{5}{12} = 1\frac{5}{12}$$
$$\overline{}\ 3\frac{1}{12}$$

$$1\frac{1}{12}$$
$$+ 1\frac{2}{12}$$

$$1 + \frac{7}{8} = \frac{15}{8} = 1\frac{7}{8}$$

$$1\frac{2}{3} = \frac{4}{6}$$
$$+ 1\frac{1}{2} = \frac{3}{6}$$

$$\frac{5}{8}$$
$$\frac{3}{8}$$
$$+ \frac{7}{8}$$
$$\overline{\frac{15}{8}}$$

$$\frac{8}{8}(1) + \frac{5}{8} + \frac{3}{8} + \frac{1}{8} = \frac{17}{8} = 2\frac{1}{8}$$

$$\frac{7}{8} + \frac{7}{8} + \frac{3}{8} = \frac{17}{8} = 2\frac{1}{8}$$

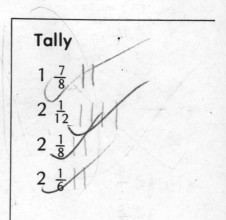

$$\frac{1}{6}$$
$$\frac{1}{6}$$
$$\frac{5}{6}$$
$$\frac{5}{6}$$
$$+ \frac{1}{6}$$

$$\frac{11}{12}$$
$$\frac{11}{12}$$
$$+ \frac{1}{4}$$

Tally

$$1\frac{7}{8} \quad ||$$
$$2\frac{1}{12} \quad ||||$$
$$2\frac{1}{8} \quad ||||$$
$$2\frac{1}{6} \quad ||$$

Fractions

Find the Sums

Reduce your answers to lowest terms when necessary.

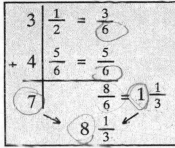

$3 \frac{1}{2} = \frac{3}{6}$

$+ 4 \frac{5}{6} = \frac{5}{6}$

7 $\frac{8}{6} = 1\frac{1}{3}$

$8 \frac{1}{3}$

$3 \frac{2}{5} \frac{2}{52} \frac{4}{10}$
$+ 6 \frac{3}{10} \frac{3}{10}$
$9 \frac{1}{10}$ ✓

$4 \frac{5}{12} \frac{5}{12}$
$+ 2 \frac{5}{6} \frac{10}{12}$
$6 \frac{5}{12} 6\frac{3}{12}$

$4 \frac{4}{7} \frac{72}{126}$
$9 \frac{2}{3} \frac{84}{126}$
$+ 5 \frac{5}{6} \frac{105}{126}$
$\frac{261}{126} = 2\frac{9}{126}$

$7 \frac{7}{8} \frac{21}{24}$
$5 \frac{1}{4} \frac{6}{24}$
$+ 3 \frac{2}{3} \frac{16}{24}$
$5 \frac{3}{24}$

$12 \frac{5}{7} \frac{120}{168}$
$39 \frac{5}{6} \frac{140}{168}$
$+ 17 \frac{3}{4} \frac{126}{168}$
$\frac{386}{168} = \frac{193}{84}$

$13 \frac{4}{5} \frac{96}{120}$
$38 \frac{3}{8} \frac{45}{120}$
$+ 18 \frac{2}{3} \frac{80}{120}$
$\frac{221}{120} \frac{101}{120}$

61

Fractions

Find the Sums

$$\frac{1}{2} \quad \frac{3}{8} \qquad \frac{2}{3} \quad \frac{5}{12}$$
$$\frac{1}{4} \quad \frac{1}{4} \qquad \frac{1}{4} \quad \frac{1}{4}$$
$$+\frac{3}{8} \quad +\frac{1}{2} \qquad +\frac{5}{12} \quad +\frac{2}{3}$$

(handwritten: $\frac{4}{8}\ \frac{2}{8}\ \frac{3}{8}\ \frac{9}{8}=1\frac{1}{8}$) (handwritten: $\frac{9}{8}=1\frac{1}{8}$) (handwritten: $\frac{8}{12}\ \frac{3}{12}\ \frac{5}{12}\ \frac{16}{12}=1\frac{4}{12}$) (handwritten: $\frac{16}{12}=1\frac{4}{12}$)

$$8\frac{2}{5} \quad 3\frac{1}{6} \qquad 6\frac{1}{2} \quad 9\frac{3}{4}$$
$$2\frac{3}{10} \quad 2\frac{3}{10} \qquad 5\frac{2}{3} \quad 5\frac{2}{3}$$
$$+3\frac{1}{6} \quad +8\frac{2}{5} \qquad +9\frac{3}{4} \quad +6\frac{1}{2}$$

(handwritten: $\frac{12}{30}\ \frac{9}{30}\ \frac{5}{30}\ 13\frac{26}{30}$) (handwritten: $13\frac{26}{30}$) (handwritten: $\frac{6}{12}\ \frac{8}{12}\ \frac{9}{12}\ \frac{23}{12}=1\frac{11}{12}$) (handwritten: $\frac{23}{12}=1\frac{11}{12}$)

$$4\frac{2}{3} \quad 6\frac{2}{5} \qquad 9\frac{3}{4} \quad 3\frac{1}{5}$$
$$2\frac{4}{15} \quad 2\frac{4}{15} \qquad 7\frac{2}{3} \quad 7\frac{2}{3}$$
$$+6\frac{2}{5} \quad +4\frac{2}{3} \qquad +3\frac{1}{5} \quad +9\frac{3}{4}$$

(handwritten: $\frac{10}{15}\ \frac{6}{15}\ 12\frac{20}{15}=13\frac{5}{15}$) (handwritten: $12\frac{20}{15}=2\frac{5}{5}$) (handwritten: $\frac{45}{60}\ \frac{40}{60}\ \frac{12}{60}\ \frac{97}{60}$) (handwritten: $\frac{97}{60}$)

The Homework Booklet

Fractions — 3 points

Fractions and Mixed Numbers

Find the differences.

$$\frac{3}{4} = \frac{15}{20}$$
$$-\frac{2}{5} = \frac{8}{20}$$
$$\frac{7}{20}$$

$$\frac{4}{5} = \frac{12}{15}$$
$$-\frac{2}{3} = \frac{10}{15}$$
$$\frac{2}{15}$$

$$\frac{2}{3} = \frac{8}{12}$$
$$-\frac{1}{4} = \frac{3}{12}$$
$$\frac{5}{12}$$

$$\frac{7}{8} = \frac{21}{24}$$
$$-\frac{5}{6} = \frac{20}{24}$$
$$\frac{1}{24}$$

$$\frac{3}{5} = \frac{27}{45}$$
$$-\frac{4}{9} = \frac{20}{45}$$
$$\frac{7}{45}$$

$$\frac{8}{9} = \frac{32}{36}$$
$$-\frac{3}{4} = \frac{27}{36}$$
$$\frac{5}{36}$$

$$\frac{5}{7} = \frac{15}{21}$$
$$-\frac{1}{3} = \frac{7}{21}$$

$$\frac{8}{21}$$

$$\frac{2}{3} = \frac{22}{33}$$
$$-\frac{5}{11} = \frac{15}{33}$$
$$\frac{7}{33}$$

63

'o point **Fractions**

Find the Differences

Reduce your answers if necessary.

$$1\tfrac{1}{2} = \tfrac{3}{2} = \tfrac{12}{8}$$
$$-\ \tfrac{7}{8} = \qquad \tfrac{7}{8}$$
$$\tfrac{5}{8}$$

$$1\tfrac{1}{3} = \tfrac{5}{15} = \tfrac{20}{15}$$
$$-\ \tfrac{4}{5} = \tfrac{12}{5} = \tfrac{12}{15}$$
$$\tfrac{8}{15}$$

$$1\tfrac{1}{12} = \tfrac{1}{12} = \tfrac{13}{12}$$
$$-\ \tfrac{5}{6} = \tfrac{10}{2} = \tfrac{10}{12}$$
$$\tfrac{3}{12} = \tfrac{1}{4}$$

$$1\tfrac{3}{4} = \tfrac{9}{12} = \tfrac{21}{12}$$
$$-\ \tfrac{11}{12} = \tfrac{11}{12} = \tfrac{11}{12}$$
$$\tfrac{10}{12} = \tfrac{5}{6}$$

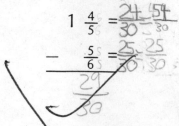

$$1\tfrac{4}{5} = \tfrac{24}{30} = \tfrac{54}{30}$$
$$-\ \tfrac{5}{6} = \tfrac{25}{30} = \tfrac{25}{30}$$
$$\tfrac{29}{30}$$

$$1\tfrac{1}{8} = \tfrac{1}{8} = \tfrac{9}{8}$$
$$-\ \tfrac{1}{2} = \tfrac{4}{8} = \tfrac{4}{8}$$
$$\tfrac{5}{8}$$

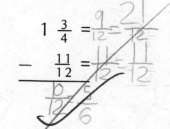

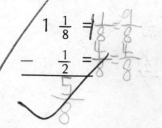

$$1\tfrac{2}{3} = \tfrac{16}{24} = \tfrac{40}{24}$$
$$-\ \tfrac{7}{8} = \tfrac{21}{24} = \tfrac{21}{24}$$
$$\tfrac{19}{24}$$

$$1\tfrac{13}{5} = \tfrac{3}{15} = \tfrac{18}{15}$$
$$-\ \tfrac{15}{3} = \tfrac{5}{15} = \tfrac{5}{15}$$
$$\tfrac{13}{15}$$

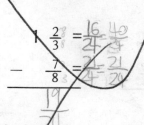

64

Fractions

2 points

Find the Differences

Reduce your answers if necessary.

$$1\frac{1}{4} = \frac{5}{4} = \frac{25}{20}$$
$$-\ \frac{4}{5} = \frac{16}{20}$$
$$\frac{9}{20}$$

$$1\frac{1}{5} = \frac{3}{15} = \frac{18}{15}$$
$$-\ \frac{2}{3} = \frac{10}{15} = \frac{10}{15}$$
$$\frac{8}{15}$$

$$1\frac{1}{2} = \frac{3}{6} = \frac{9}{6}$$
$$-\ \frac{5}{6} = \frac{5}{6} = \frac{5}{6}$$
$$\frac{4}{6}\ \frac{2}{6}$$

$$1\frac{1}{12} = \frac{2}{24} = \frac{26}{24}$$
$$-\ \frac{3}{8} = \frac{9}{24} = \frac{9}{24}$$
$$\frac{17}{24}$$

$$1\frac{7}{8} = \frac{21}{24} = \frac{45}{24}$$
$$-\ \frac{11}{12} = \frac{22}{24} = \frac{22}{24}$$
$$\frac{23}{24}$$

$$1\frac{2}{3} = \frac{14}{21} = \frac{35}{21}$$
$$-\ \frac{6}{7} = \frac{18}{21} = \frac{18}{21}$$
$$\frac{17}{21}$$

$$1\frac{1}{8} = \frac{5}{40} = \frac{45}{40}$$
$$-\ \frac{3}{5} = \frac{24}{40} = \frac{24}{40}$$
$$\frac{21}{40}$$

$$1\frac{1}{3} = \frac{8}{24} = \frac{32}{24}$$
$$-\ \frac{7}{8} = \frac{21}{24} = \frac{21}{24}$$
$$\frac{11}{24}$$

65

© 1984, Instructional Fair, Inc.

1 points (handwritten)

Fractions

Find the Differences

Reduce your answers if necessary.

$$2\frac{1}{2} = \left(\frac{5}{10} + \frac{10}{10}\right)\frac{15}{10}$$
$$-\ \frac{3}{5} = \hspace{3cm} \frac{6}{10}$$
$$\overline{1 \hspace{3.5cm} \frac{9}{10}}$$
$$1\frac{9}{10}$$

$$3\frac{2}{5} = \frac{6}{15} = 8\frac{21}{15}$$
$$-\ \frac{2}{3} = \frac{10}{15} = \frac{10}{15}$$
$$\overline{2\frac{11}{15}}$$

$$6\frac{1}{8} = 6\frac{1}{8} 5\frac{9}{8}$$
$$-\ \frac{3}{4} = \frac{6}{8} = \frac{6}{8}$$
$$\overline{5\frac{3}{8}}$$

$$2\frac{3}{5} = \frac{18}{30} = \frac{48}{30}$$
$$-\ \frac{5}{6} = \frac{25}{30} = \frac{25}{30}$$
$$\overline{\frac{23}{30}}$$

$$4\frac{1}{5} = \frac{8}{40} = \frac{48}{40}$$
$$-\ \frac{3}{8} = \frac{15}{40} = \frac{15}{40}$$
$$\overline{3\frac{33}{40}}$$

The Homework Booklet

Fractions

− 1 points

Fractions and Mixed Numbers

Find the differences.

$$\begin{array}{r} \overset{3}{\cancel{4}}\,\frac{1}{10} = \left(\frac{1}{10} + \frac{10}{10}\right) = \frac{11}{10} \\ -\ 2\,\frac{3}{5} = \qquad\qquad \frac{6}{10} \\ \hline 1 \qquad\qquad \frac{5}{10} = \frac{1}{2} \end{array}$$

$$1\,\frac{1}{2}$$

study this first

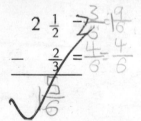

$2\frac{1}{2} = \frac{3}{6} \quad \frac{9}{6}$

$-\ \ \frac{2}{3} = \frac{4}{6} \quad \frac{4}{6}$

$\frac{5}{6}$

$3\frac{2}{5} = \frac{12}{30} \quad \frac{42}{30}$

$-\ \ \frac{5}{6} = \frac{25}{30} \quad \frac{25}{30}$

$\frac{17}{30}$

$7\frac{1}{8} = 7\frac{3}{24} \quad \frac{6}{24} \quad \frac{27}{24}$

$-\ 2\frac{1}{3} = 2\frac{8}{24} \quad 2\frac{8}{24}$

$\frac{4}{24}$

$9\frac{1}{3} = 7\frac{94}{12} \quad \frac{16}{12}$

$-\ 5\frac{3}{4} = 5\frac{9}{12} \quad 5\frac{9}{12}$

$3\frac{7}{12}$

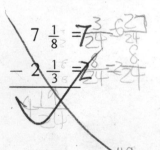

$4\frac{27}{57} = \frac{14}{35} \quad \frac{49}{35}$

$-\ 2\frac{45}{75} = \frac{20}{35} \quad \frac{20}{35}$

$\frac{29}{35}$

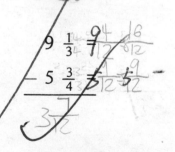

$6\frac{3}{42} = \frac{6}{8} \quad \frac{14}{8}$

$-\ 5\frac{7}{8} = \frac{7}{8} \quad \frac{7}{8}$

$\frac{7}{8}$

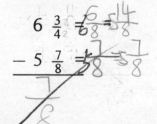

67

© 1984, Instructional Fair, Inc.

Fractions

Fractions and Mixed Numbers

Find the differences.

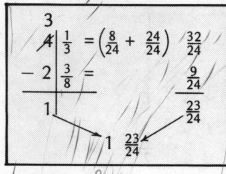

$$\begin{array}{l} \overset{3}{\cancel{4}}\ \frac{1}{3} = \left(\frac{8}{24} + \frac{24}{24}\right)\ \frac{32}{24} \\ -\ 2\ \frac{3}{8} = \qquad\qquad\ \frac{9}{24} \\ \hline 1 \qquad\qquad\qquad\quad \frac{23}{24} \end{array}$$

$$1\ \frac{23}{24}$$

— 3 points

$$2\ \frac{1}{5} = \frac{8}{40} = \frac{48}{40}$$
$$-\ \ \frac{3}{8} = \frac{15}{40} = \frac{15}{40}$$
$$\overline{\quad\ \frac{33}{40}\quad}$$

$$4\ \frac{15}{35} = \frac{5}{15} = \frac{20}{15}$$
$$-\ 1\ \frac{2}{5} = \frac{6}{15} = \frac{6}{15}$$
$$\overline{\ 2\frac{14}{15} = \frac{1}{15}\ }$$

$$5\ \frac{14}{64} = \frac{4}{24} = \frac{28}{24}$$
$$-\ 2\ \frac{36}{40} = \frac{18}{24} = \frac{18}{24}$$
$$\overline{\ \frac{10}{24} = \frac{5}{12}\ }$$

$$6\ \frac{22}{72} = \frac{4}{14} = \frac{18}{14}$$
$$-\ 4\ \frac{17}{2} = \frac{7}{14} = \frac{7}{14}$$
$$\overline{\ 1\frac{11}{14}\ }$$

$$12\ \frac{27}{31} = \frac{14}{21} = \frac{35}{21}$$
$$-\ 9\ \frac{63}{7} = \frac{18}{21} = \frac{18}{21}$$
$$\overline{\quad \frac{7}{21}\quad}$$

$$5\ \frac{14}{64} = \frac{4}{24} = \frac{28}{24}$$
$$-\ 2\ \frac{36}{4} = \frac{18}{24} = \frac{18}{24}$$
$$\overline{\ \frac{10}{24} = \frac{5}{12}\ }$$

Fraction Tic-Tac-Toe

Math Puzzles

Work each problem. Write the answers in the corresponding spaces on the square below.

a. $\dfrac{1}{4} \cdot \dfrac{1}{6} = \dfrac{10}{24} \to \dfrac{5}{12}$

b. $\dfrac{1}{2} + \dfrac{1}{3} = \dfrac{5}{6}$

c. $\dfrac{1}{2} - \dfrac{1}{4} = \dfrac{1}{4}$

d. $\dfrac{1}{2} - \dfrac{1}{6} = \dfrac{2}{6} = \dfrac{1}{3}$

e. $\dfrac{1}{3} + \dfrac{1}{6} = \dfrac{3}{6} = \dfrac{1}{2}$

f. $\dfrac{1}{6} + \dfrac{1}{2} = \dfrac{4}{6} = \dfrac{2}{3}$

g. $\dfrac{5}{6} - \dfrac{1}{12} = \dfrac{9}{12} = \dfrac{3}{4}$

h. $\dfrac{1}{2} - \dfrac{1}{3} = \dfrac{1}{6}$

i. $\dfrac{1}{4} + \dfrac{1}{3} = \dfrac{7}{12}$

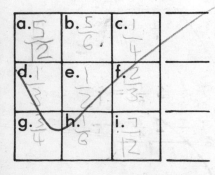

a. $\dfrac{5}{12}$	b. $\dfrac{5}{6}$	c. $\dfrac{1}{4}$
d. $\dfrac{1}{3}$	e. $\dfrac{1}{2}$	f. $\dfrac{2}{3}$
g. $\dfrac{3}{4}$	h. $\dfrac{1}{6}$	i. $\dfrac{7}{12}$

Add every row, every column, and both diagonals. If your answers are correct, all totals will be the same.

69

~ 6 point **Fractions**

Fractions and Mixed Numbers

Find the sum or difference.

$\frac{42}{52} = \frac{8}{10}$

$+ \ \frac{15}{25} = \frac{5}{10}$

$\frac{13}{10} = 1\frac{3}{10}$ ✓

$\frac{15}{17}$

$- \ \frac{8}{17}$

$\frac{7}{17}$ ✓

$\frac{3}{4} = \frac{21}{28}$

$+ \ \frac{54}{74} = \frac{20}{28}$

$\frac{41}{28} = 1\frac{13}{28}$ ✗

$4\ \frac{15}{25} = \frac{5}{10}$

$+\ 2\ \frac{32}{52} = \frac{6}{10}$

$6\frac{11}{10} = 7\frac{1}{10}$

$8\ \frac{38}{58} = \frac{24}{40} = \frac{64}{40}$

$-\ 6\ \frac{75}{85} = \frac{35}{40} = \frac{25}{40}$

$\frac{29}{40}$ ✓

$\frac{153}{163} = \frac{45}{48}$

$-\ \frac{74}{124} = \frac{28}{48}$

$\frac{17}{48}$ ✓

$\frac{5}{7}$

$+\ \frac{3}{7}$

$\frac{8}{7} = 1\frac{1}{7}$ ✓

$\frac{55}{85} = \frac{25}{40}$

$+\ \frac{74}{10} = \frac{28}{40}$

$\frac{53}{40} = 1\frac{13}{40}$

$\frac{31}{35}$

$-\ \frac{16}{35}$

$\frac{15}{35}$ 3

$7\ \frac{2}{3} = \frac{10}{15}\ \ \frac{25}{}$

$-\ 3\ \frac{4}{5} = \frac{12}{15} = \frac{12}{15}$

$3\frac{13}{15}$ ✓

The Homework Booklet

Fractions

Find the Sums

Check by subtracting.

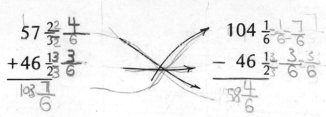

$57 \frac{22}{32} \frac{4}{6}$
$+46 \frac{13}{23} \frac{3}{6}$
$103 \frac{7}{6}$

$104 \frac{1}{6} \frac{17}{6} \frac{7}{6}$
$- 46 \frac{13}{23} \frac{3}{6} \frac{3}{6}$
$58 \frac{4}{6}$

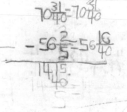

$14 \frac{3}{8} \frac{15}{40}$
$+56 \frac{2}{5} \frac{28}{40} \frac{16}{40}$
$70 \frac{31}{40}$

$70 \frac{31}{40} = 70 \frac{31}{40}$
$- 56 \frac{2}{5} = 56 \frac{16}{40}$
$14 \frac{15}{40}$

$77 \frac{3}{4} \frac{15}{20}$
$+49 \frac{7}{10} \frac{14}{20}$
$126 \frac{29}{20}$

$126 \frac{29}{20} = 126 \frac{29}{20}$
$-49 \frac{7}{10} = 49 \frac{14}{20}$
$77 \frac{15}{20}$

$98 \frac{7}{16} \frac{7}{16}$
$+26 \frac{5}{8} \frac{10}{16}$
$124 \frac{17}{16} = 1 \frac{1}{16}$

$124 \frac{17}{16} = \frac{17}{16}$
$- 26 \frac{5}{8} \frac{10}{16}$
$98 \frac{7}{16}$ ✓

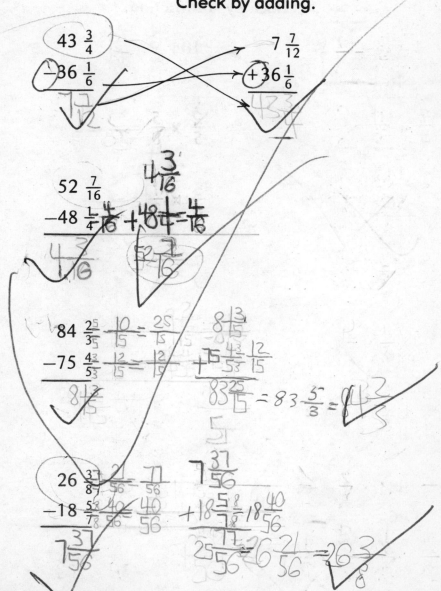

Fractions

—5 points

Find the Differences

Check by adding.

$43 \frac{3}{4}$ $7 \frac{7}{12}$

$-36 \frac{1}{6}$ $+36 \frac{1}{6}$

$52 \frac{7}{16}$ $4\frac{3}{16}$

$-48 \frac{1}{4}$ $+48$ $52\frac{7}{16}$

$84 \frac{25}{35} = \frac{10}{15} = \frac{25}{15}$ $8\frac{13}{15}$

$-75 \frac{43}{53} = \frac{12}{15} = \frac{12}{15}$ $+75\frac{43}{53} \frac{12}{15}$

$83\frac{25}{15} = 83\frac{5}{3} = 84\frac{2}{5}$

$26 \frac{37}{8} \frac{21}{56} = \frac{77}{56}$ $7\frac{37}{56}$

$-18 \frac{53}{78} \frac{40}{56} = \frac{40}{56}$ $+18\frac{5}{8} \frac{8}{18} = 18\frac{40}{56}$

$25\frac{77}{56} = 6\frac{21}{56} = 26\frac{3}{8}$

The Homework Booklet   ©1984, Instructional Fair, Inc.

Fractions

Find the Products

Cancel where possible.

$$\frac{3}{4} \times \frac{1}{3} = \frac{1}{4}$$

$$\frac{5}{6} \times \frac{3}{8} = \frac{5}{16}$$

$$\frac{2}{5} \times \frac{1}{3} = \frac{2}{5}$$

$$\frac{2}{5} \times \frac{5}{8} = \frac{5}{20}$$

$$\frac{9}{10} \times \frac{2}{3} = \frac{3}{5}$$

$$\frac{5}{6} \times \frac{1}{3} = \frac{5}{18}$$

$$\frac{5}{8} \times \frac{3}{5} = \frac{3}{8}$$

$$\frac{7}{9} \times \frac{1}{4} = \frac{7}{36}$$

$$\frac{1}{3} \times \frac{4}{5} = $$

$$\frac{3}{8} \times \frac{5}{12} = \frac{5}{32}$$

$$\frac{3}{4} \times \frac{5}{8} = 5$$

$$\frac{2}{7} \times \frac{14}{15} = \frac{2}{5}$$

$$\frac{4}{5} \times \frac{3}{4} \times \frac{2}{3} = \frac{2}{5}$$

$$\frac{3}{16} \times \frac{1}{2} \times \frac{1}{3} = \frac{1}{3}$$

$$\frac{3}{7} \times \frac{5}{6} \times \frac{14}{15} = \frac{1}{3}$$

$$\frac{5}{8} \times \frac{11}{12} \times \frac{9}{10} = \frac{33}{64}$$

73

~ 2 points **Fractions**

Find the Products

Cancel where possible.

Here's how

$$\frac{\overset{1}{\cancel{2}}}{5} \times \frac{3}{\cancel{4}_2} = \frac{3}{10}$$

$$\frac{3}{8} \times \frac{8}{10} = \frac{3}{10}$$

$$\frac{5}{6} \times \frac{3}{4} = \frac{5}{8}$$

$$\frac{9}{16} \times \frac{5}{6} = \frac{15}{3}$$

$$\frac{7}{10} \times \frac{3}{5} = \frac{21}{50}$$

$$\frac{4}{7} \times \frac{1}{6} = \frac{2}{21}$$

$$\frac{2}{3} \times \frac{7}{8} = \frac{7}{12}$$

$$\frac{5}{9} \times \frac{3}{5} = \frac{1}{3}$$

$$\frac{3}{4} \times \frac{3}{5} = \frac{9}{20}$$

$$\frac{3}{4} \times \frac{4}{9} = \frac{1}{3}$$

$$\frac{5}{6} \times \frac{4}{5} = \frac{2}{3}$$

$$\frac{7}{12} \times \frac{5}{6} = \frac{35}{72}$$

$$\frac{6}{7} \times \frac{2}{3} \times \frac{3}{5} = \frac{12}{35}$$

$$\frac{5}{8} \times \frac{4}{5} \times \frac{1}{2} = \frac{4}{16} = \frac{1}{4}$$

$$\frac{3}{5} \times \frac{8}{9} \times \frac{5}{6} = \frac{4}{9}$$

$$\frac{25}{42} \times \frac{18}{25} \times \frac{2}{3} = \frac{12}{42}$$

74

Number Table

Complete the Table

×	$\frac{3}{5}$	$\frac{1}{2}$	$\frac{2}{3}$	$\frac{1}{6}$	$\frac{1}{8}$
$\frac{1}{2}$	$\frac{3}{10}$		$\frac{1}{3}$		
$\frac{3}{8}$	$\frac{9}{40}$	$\frac{3}{16}$			$\frac{3}{64}$
$\frac{4}{7}$	$\frac{12}{35}$	$\frac{2}{7}$	$\frac{8}{21}$	$\frac{2}{21}$	$\frac{1}{14}$
$\frac{5}{8}$	$\frac{3}{8}$	$\frac{5}{16}$	$\frac{5}{12}$	$\frac{5}{48}$	$\frac{5}{64}$
$\frac{1}{10}$	$\frac{3}{50}$	$\frac{1}{20}$	$\frac{1}{15}$		$\frac{1}{80}$

75

Fractions

Find the Products

Cancel where possible.

$$3\frac{1}{3} \times 2\frac{3}{4} = \frac{\overset{5}{\cancel{10}}}{3} \times \frac{11}{\underset{2}{\cancel{4}}} = \frac{55}{6} = 9\frac{1}{6}$$

$2\frac{2}{3} \times \frac{3}{4} =$

$4\frac{2}{3} \times 5\frac{1}{4} =$

$3\frac{3}{4} \times 5\frac{7}{9} =$

$6\frac{2}{5} \times 2\frac{1}{2} =$

$5\frac{1}{5} \times 3\frac{1}{2} =$

$3\frac{1}{2} \times 3\frac{3}{4} =$

$5\frac{5}{9} \times 5\frac{1}{4} =$

$4\frac{5}{8} \times 2\frac{4}{5} =$

$5\frac{4}{7} \times 4\frac{1}{5} =$

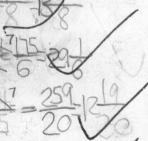

Fractions

Find the Quotients

Cancel where possible.

$$\frac{5}{6} \div \frac{3}{10} = \frac{5}{\underset{3}{\cancel{6}}} \times \frac{\overset{5}{\cancel{10}}}{3} = \frac{25}{9} = 2\frac{7}{9}$$

Here's an example

$$\frac{3}{4} \div \frac{1}{3} = \frac{3}{4} \times \frac{3}{1} = \frac{9}{4} = 2\frac{1}{4}$$

$$\frac{5}{6} \div \frac{3}{8} = \frac{5}{\underset{3}{\cancel{6}}} \times \frac{\overset{4}{\cancel{8}}}{3} = \frac{20}{9} = 2\frac{2}{9}$$

$$\frac{2}{5} \div \frac{1}{3} = \frac{2}{5} \times \frac{3}{1} = \frac{6}{5} = 1\frac{1}{5}$$

$$\frac{5}{6} \div \frac{1}{3} = \frac{5}{\underset{2}{\cancel{6}}} \times \frac{\cancel{3}}{1} = \frac{5}{2} = 2\frac{1}{2}$$

$$\frac{5}{8} \div \frac{3}{5} = \frac{5}{8} \times \frac{5}{3} = \frac{25}{24} = 1\frac{1}{24}$$

$$\frac{3}{8} \div \frac{1}{6} = \frac{3}{8} \times \frac{6}{1} = \frac{18}{8} = 2\frac{2}{4} = 2\frac{1}{4}$$

$$\frac{3}{4} \div \frac{5}{8} = \frac{3}{\underset{1}{\cancel{4}}} \times \frac{\overset{2}{\cancel{8}}}{5} = \frac{6}{5} = 1\frac{1}{5}$$

$$\frac{9}{16} \div \frac{1}{2} = \frac{9}{\underset{8}{\cancel{16}}} \times \frac{\cancel{2}}{1} = \frac{9}{8} = 1\frac{1}{8}$$

77

Fractions

8 points

Find the Quotients

Cancel where possible.

$$\frac{3}{10} \div \frac{5}{6} = \frac{3}{10} \times \frac{\cancel{6}^3}{5} = \frac{9}{25}$$

$\frac{4}{5} \div \frac{5}{8} =$

$\frac{9}{10} \div \frac{2}{3} =$

$\frac{7}{9} \div \frac{1}{4} =$

$\frac{3}{5} \div \frac{5}{9} =$

$\frac{7}{9} \div \frac{3}{5} =$

$\frac{6}{7} \div \frac{14}{15} =$

$\frac{4}{5} \div \frac{3}{4} =$

$\frac{6}{7} \div \frac{2}{7} =$

Fractions 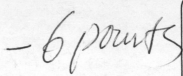 — 6 points

Find the Quotients

Cancel where possible.

$$3\frac{1}{2} \div 2\frac{3}{8} = \frac{7}{2} \div \frac{19}{8} = \frac{7}{2} \times \frac{\overset{4}{\cancel{8}}}{\underset{1}{19}} = \frac{28}{19} = 1\frac{9}{19}$$

$3\frac{3}{5} \div 3\frac{3}{4} = \frac{\overset{6}{\cancel{18}}}{5} \times \frac{4}{\cancel{15}_5} = \frac{24}{25}$

$2\frac{1}{2} \div 3\frac{8}{9} =$

$4\frac{2}{3} \div 5\frac{9}{10} = \frac{14}{3} \times \frac{10}{59} = \frac{140}{11}$

$6\frac{3}{8} \div 2\frac{5}{6} = \frac{\cancel{51}}{8_4} \times \frac{\cancel{6}}{17_1} = \frac{9}{4}$

$3\frac{3}{5} \div 2\frac{4}{5} = \frac{\overset{9}{\cancel{18}}}{5_1} \times \frac{\cancel{5}}{14_7} = \frac{9}{7} = 1\frac{2}{7}$

$9\frac{3}{8} \div 4\frac{5}{12} = \frac{75}{8_2} \times \frac{\cancel{12}}{53} = \frac{225}{106} = 2\frac{13}{106}$

$5\frac{1}{2} \div 1\frac{1}{8} = \frac{11}{8_1} \times \frac{\cancel{8}^4}{9} = \frac{44}{9} = 4\frac{8}{9}$

$6\frac{1}{3} \div 3\frac{5}{6} = \frac{19}{3_1} \times \frac{\cancel{6}}{23} = \frac{38}{23} = 1\frac{15}{23}$

The Homework Booklet

Fractions

— 6 points

Find the Quotients

Cancel where possible.

— 5 pom

$$2\frac{3}{8} \div 3\frac{1}{2} = \frac{19}{8} \div \frac{7}{2} = \frac{19}{\underset{4}{8}} \times \frac{2}{7} = \frac{19}{28}$$

$2\frac{3}{5} \div 3\frac{7}{20} =$

$3\frac{1}{3} \div 5\frac{3}{5} =$

$5\frac{2}{5} \div 6\frac{5}{8} =$

$4\frac{3}{8} \div 3\frac{3}{5} =$

$4\frac{1}{7} \div 2\frac{3}{7} =$

$7\frac{1}{9} \div 5\frac{1}{3} =$

$6\frac{3}{4} \div 2\frac{5}{8} =$

$9\frac{3}{5} \div 8\frac{2}{3} =$

Fractions

6 points

Find the Product or Quotient

Cancel where possible.

$\frac{4}{7} \times \frac{1}{2} =$

$\frac{8}{15} \times \frac{3}{10} =$

$4\frac{4}{7} \times 3\frac{3}{8} =$

$5\frac{5}{8} \times 2\frac{7}{10} =$

$4\frac{2}{7} \times 1\frac{7}{10} =$

$\frac{3}{5} \div \frac{1}{2} =$

$\frac{7}{10} \div \frac{3}{5} =$

$2\frac{5}{6} \div 5\frac{1}{10} =$

$5\frac{1}{4} \div 2\frac{1}{3} =$

$7\frac{3}{8} \div 1\frac{5}{16} =$

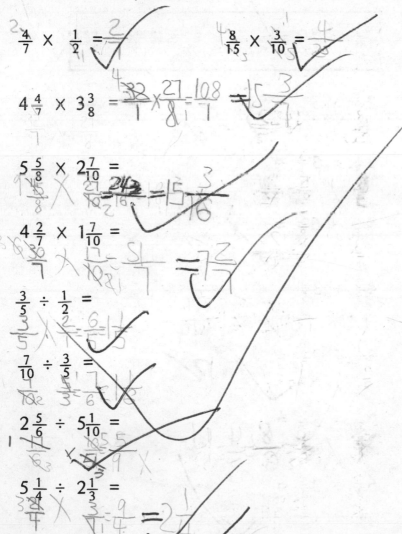

81

—4 points **Fractions**

Find the Product or Quotient

Cancel where possible.

$$\frac{7}{16} \times \frac{8}{9} = $$
$$\frac{14}{27} \times \frac{3}{16} = $$

$$3\frac{3}{15} \times 6\frac{2}{8} = $$

$$7\frac{1}{5} \times 3\frac{1}{4} = $$

$$8\frac{1}{10} \times 1\frac{5}{9} = $$

$$\frac{6}{7} \div \frac{2}{9} = $$

$$\frac{7}{8} \div \frac{3}{16} = $$

$$6\frac{3}{10} \div 2\frac{2}{5} = $$

$$4\frac{5}{12} \div 1\frac{5}{18} = $$

$$3\frac{1}{2} \div 4\frac{5}{6} = $$

©1984, Instructional Fair, Inc.

Fractions

Find the Products

Check by dividing.

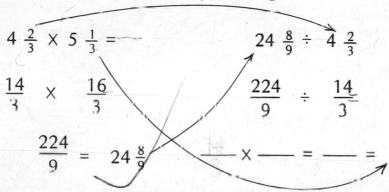

$$4 \frac{2}{3} \times 5 \frac{1}{3} = \underline{\quad} \qquad 24 \frac{8}{9} \div 4 \frac{2}{3}$$

$$\frac{14}{3} \times \frac{16}{3} \qquad\qquad \frac{224}{9} \div \frac{14}{3}$$

$$\frac{224}{9} = 24 \frac{8}{9} \qquad \underline{\quad} \times \underline{\quad} = \underline{\quad} =$$

$$6 \frac{3}{4} \times 7 \frac{5}{8} = \underline{\quad}$$

$$\frac{27}{4} \times \frac{61}{8} = \frac{1647}{32} = 22 \frac{514}{32} = 24 \frac{16}{32}$$

$$211 \frac{16}{}$$

$$2 \frac{1}{2} \times 10 \frac{2}{3} =$$

$$\frac{5}{2} \qquad \frac{32}{3} = \frac{160}{6} = 4 \frac{26}{6} = 6 \frac{4}{6} = 6 \frac{2}{3}$$

Fractions

Find the Quotients

Check by multiplying.

$10\frac{1}{2} \div 2 =$ $2 \times 5\frac{1}{4} =$

$\frac{21}{2} \div \frac{2}{1}$ $\frac{1}{\frac{2}{1}} \times \frac{21}{4} =$

$\frac{21}{2} \times \frac{1}{2} = \frac{21}{4} = 5\frac{1}{4}$ 2

$12\frac{2}{3} \div 4 = 12\frac{2}{12} = 12\frac{1}{6}$

$\frac{8}{4} \times 12\frac{2}{8} = \frac{2}{3}$

$34 \div 3\frac{2}{5} = 3\frac{\square}{2}\frac{Q}{2}$

$3\frac{8}{5} \times 3\frac{17}{8} = 9\frac{10}{34}$

$8\frac{2}{3} \div 2\frac{2}{3} = 16\frac{6}{6}$

$16\frac{8}{6} \times 2\frac{8}{8} = 16\frac{2}{3}$

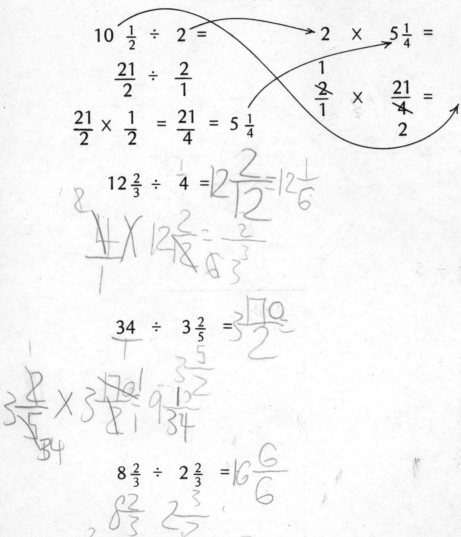

Math Puzzles

What solution is named most often? _____

$$\frac{1}{4} \div \frac{1}{3} \quad \frac{3}{4}$$

$$\frac{5}{6} - 1\frac{1}{2} = \frac{2}{6} \cdot \frac{1}{3}$$

$$\frac{7}{8} \times \frac{4}{7} \quad \frac{1}{2}$$

$$\frac{5}{12} + \frac{1}{4} = \frac{2}{12} \cdot \frac{1}{6}$$

$$1\frac{1}{1} - \frac{1}{2} \quad \frac{1}{2}$$

$$\frac{1}{5} + \frac{3}{10} \quad \frac{5}{10} \cdot \frac{1}{2}$$

$$\frac{2}{15} \div \frac{2}{5} \quad \frac{1}{3}$$

$$1\frac{2}{3} \div 5 = \frac{2}{15}$$

$$\frac{1}{6} \div \frac{1}{3} = \frac{2}{6} \cdot \frac{1}{3}$$

$$\frac{5}{6} \times \frac{2}{5} = \frac{10}{3}$$

Tally	
$\frac{1}{3}$	|||||
$\frac{1}{2}$	|||
$\frac{2}{3}$	
$\frac{3}{4}$	|

85

Crosswords

Write the word that corresponds to each clue on the correct spaces on the puzzle.

1. 2/7; 2 is the _____.
2. 5/2 is an _____ fraction.
3. 3½ is a _____ number.
4. 7/8 is in _____ terms.
5. 3/6 will _____ to ½.
6. 2/7; 7 is the _____ .

You have finished this Book

©1984, Instructional Fair, Inc.